TASTE THE *World*

A BOULEVARD MARKET
ALMANAC OF COOKING

BY ERIKA AYLWARD

TASTE THE *World*

A BOULEVARD MARKET
ALMANAC OF COOKING

**WRITTEN BY
ERIKA AYLWARD**

**PHOTOGRAPHY BY
SARAH CHINAVARE**

ABOUT THE AUTHOR

Welcome! 20 years ago I founded The Boulevard Market with my husband and daughters. A beautiful historic building in downtown Tecumseh Michigan became our opportunity to create, learn, share and explore the world of traditional cheese, food & wine. It allowed us to become producers of fine food as well.

We've felt so fortunate to be a part of a vibrant community that supports our Market and warmly welcomes our global suppliers.

John and I have been able to travel and experience global cuisines and culture and share those stories, ideas and products with our customers.

This volume of "Taste The World" is a collection of a few of our favorite recipes and travel photos. It has been brought to life through a collaboration of local women, Sarah and Nanci, that make dreams come true for all of us and share our passions with you!

- Erika Aylward

CROSTINI WITH SMOKED FRESH MOZZARELLA & ARUGULA

INGREDIENTS

1 ball smoked fresh mozzarella, sliced ¼ inch thick
1 baguette, sliced on the bias ½ inch thick
2 handfuls fresh baby arugula
Extra virgin olive oil, best quality you've got
Sea salt, big flake style like Maldon

DIRECTIONS

STEP ONE
Preheat oven to 350 degrees.
Slice baguette on the bias and toast in preheated oven about 8-10 minutes until golden brown. Remove and let cool about 5 minutes.

STEP TWO
Toss arugula with a bit of olive oil and place a small bunch on top of each baguette slice. Top arugula with a slice of fresh mozzarella. Drizzle olive oil over top of cheese and sprinkle each crostini with a generous pinch of sea salt. Serve immediately.

This simple spring bite requires the freshest ingredients and best quality olive oil and salt you can afford. You can also play with different types of salt and mixed greens for variations!

Charcuterie

"FRENCH-INSPIRED"

INGREDIENTS

Brie or similar soft cheese
Gruyere
Goat cheese (fresh chevre)
Tomme de Savoie
St Agur or favorite blue cheese
Fresh figs, edible flower blossoms, herbs, olives, baguette, prosciutto or French style salame (saucisson)
You could also include; a wedge of honeycomb, cornichons and French mustard

"BRITISH-INSPIRED"

INGREDIENTS

Red Leicester
Stilton
Mature English cheddar
Red Dragon *(a cheddar with mustard seed and beer)*
Assorted salami
Grapes
Strawberries
Chutney or jam
Whole grain mustard
Nuts, roasted & salted
Sprigs of fresh herbs

CHARCUTERIE BOARD TIPS & TRICKS

Up to 5 choices of cheeses spanning different milks and textures; soft, semi-soft, blue, and hard. Goat, cow or sheep milk. ~ 2 ounces cheese per person.

Up to 4 types of cured meats or pate. ~ 2 ounces per person.

Use different slicing techniques to create visual interest, such as cubes or triangles.

Additional items; olives, cornichons, pickled vegetables, jam, honey, mustard, crackers, breads, fresh fruit. Good pairings are contrasting flavors such as sweet/spicy, sweet/salty, rich/acid, smokey/acid.

With vibrant orange, blue and white cheeses, this British-inspired board looks as wonderful as it tastes!

ALPINE CHEESE DIP

SERVINGS: 2

INGREDIENTS

1 jar Peppadew brand mild red peppers, drained & roughly chopped
1 1/2 cups grated Gruyere cheese
2/3 cup mayonnaise *(I use Dukes)*
2 Tablespoons fresh lemon juice
3 cloves garlic, minced
Salt & Pepper to taste

DIRECTIONS

Mix all ingredients until fully combined.
Place in a shallow 6 inch dish.
Bake at 400 degrees about 15-20 minutes until golden brown and bubbly. Serve with toasted baguette slices or crackers.

GOAT CHEESE BACON CRANBERRY DIP

INGREDIENTS

6 oz fresh goat cheese
1 Tablespoon bacon, cooked and crumbled
1 Tablespoon pecans, toasted and chopped fine
1/4 cup cranberry preserves
(Terrapin Ridge brand or fruit preserves of choice)
Sprig of fresh rosemary, finely chopped

DIRECTIONS

STEP ONE
Preheat oven to 350 degrees. Find a small dish for serving that is oven proof.

STEP TWO
Blend goat cheese with bacon, pecans and rosemary. Spread mixture evenly into a small oven-proof ramekin and cover completely with preserves.

STEP THREE
Garnish with another pinch of rosemary and bake about 10 minutes until warmed through. Serve with crackers or slices of toasted crusty bread.

PIMM'S CUP

INGREDIENTS

1 part Pimm's No 1

3 parts sparkling lemonade (I like Fentiman's or Lorina)

2+ inch piece of thin cucumber peel

1 mint leaf

½ strawberry

1 orange slice

Ice

DIRECTIONS

In a highball glass add mint, strawberry and orange to bottom. Fill with ice and lay cucumber slice inside glass wall. Add Pimm's and top with lemonade.

LIMONCELLO SPRITZ

INGREDIENTS

3 ounces Prosecco, cold

2 ounces Limoncello, ice cold

1 ounce club soda or sparkling mineral water, cold

Slice of fresh lemon

Fresh mint or basil sprig

DIRECTIONS

In a large wine glass add Limoncello first and top with Prosecco. Fill glass with ice and garnishes then pour sparkling water to top off.

Notes

Non-Alcoholic

MAPLE OLD FASHIONED

INGREDIENTS

2.5 ounces Kentucky 74 or another NA Bourbon

¼ ounce pure maple syrup

¼ ounce non alcoholic orange or aromatic bitters

2 ounces brewed black tea

DIRECTIONS

Combine all ingredients with a large ice cube and stir until cold. Garnish with an orange peel twist. For a smoky edge you could also scorch the edge of the peel.

FRENCH ORCHARD SPRITZ

INGREDIENTS

1 ounce Martini & Rossi Floreale NA Vermouth

4 ounces Apple Soda

Zilch or other NA sparkling dry white wine

DIRECTIONS

Combine all ingredients in a glass and stir gently. Add an extra large ice cube and garnish with a slice of apple and sprig of fresh sage.

FANCY ICE CUBES

I've really enjoyed using large ice cubes in my drinks the last few years! They melt so slowly and are easy to make really fancy in just a few minutes. I find it's brilliant to be able to create them ahead of time when I have all the garnishes on hand. I use the 6 count silicone tray.

Here are a few tips to keep them gorgeous;

Use distilled water for crystal clear cubes
Use a combination of herbs and fruit
Use small berries as they float better
Use edible flowers in season as well

I often make multiple trays at a time and store them in Ziploc bags in the freezer

When pouring bubbly wine on ice, make sure to not pour directly onto the cube as it makes your wine flat. Pour just to the side of cube.

15

ROASTED PUMPKIN SOUP

SERVINGS: 6

INGREDIENTS

3 lb pie pumpkin, cleaned out
 OR 28 ounce can pumpkin puree
3 Tablespoons butter
½ cup shallot, chopped fine
6 cups chicken or vegetable stock
2 Tablespoon fresh chives, minced
Salt & pepper
¼ cup Parmigiano Reggiano cheese, grated
½ cup Amaretti cookies, crushed into crumbs

DIRECTIONS

STEP ONE
Roasted Pumpkin: Preheat oven to 400 degrees. Cut pumpkin into 4 quarters, cover in foil and bake about 45 minutes until tender. Scoop flesh off of the skin.

STEP TWO
In a large stock pot over medium heat, melt butter and saute shallots until tender, 6 minutes or so. Add pumpkin and allow sugars to caramelize about 10 minutes. Add the stock, salt and pepper and bring to a boil. Reduce heat to simmer and cook about 30 minutes.

STEP THREE
Puree mixture using an immersion blender until thick and smooth. Taste and adjust seasonings.

STEP FOUR
Serve each bowl with a garnish of cheese, crushed cookies and fresh chives.

SALMOREJO

SERVINGS: 4

INGREDIENTS

8 medium tomatoes
8 inches of baguette bread
1 cup extra virgin olive oil
1 clove garlic, minced
Splash of sherry vinegar
Sea salt
4 hard boiled eggs, peeled
Jamon Serrano, diced
(could substitute prosciutto)

This is a Spanish late summer cold soup is for the hottest days, using the ripest homegrown tomatoes.

DIRECTIONS

STEP ONE
Bring a small pan of water to boil. Cut a small x at the bottom of each tomato and scald them in hot water briefly. Remove tomato skins and core.

STEP TWO
In a blender or food processor, blend tomatoes until completely pureed. Remove the crust from baguette (save and make croutons!) and mix interior of bread with 1 ½ cups of tomato puree. Let sit about 5 minutes until soggy. Put mixture back into blender and process until completely pureed. Check to make sure it has a thick velvety texture. If it's too thin add a bit more bread. Don't worry if it's too thick, you can correct that in the next steps.

STEP THREE
Add vinegar, garlic and a pinch of salt. Taste and correct any seasonings.

STEP FOUR
With your machine running, pour a thin stream of the olive oil into tomato mixture until emulsified. (Now is the time to double check consistency! Add a bit of water if too thick) With machine running add 1 of the hard boiled eggs and process until smooth.

STEP FIVE
Fill shallow bowl with soup. Garnish with slices of remaining hard boiled eggs, chunks of Jamon and a drizzle of olive oil.

SAVORY CREPES
SERVINGS: 4

INGREDIENTS

CREPE BATTER
¾ cup buckwheat flour
½ cup all purpose flour
3 large eggs
1 ½ cups milk

FILLING
1 cup raclette cheese, grated
½ cup cooked bacon, chopped ½ inch
½ cup onions, cleaned and sliced thin
1 large potato, boiled until tender, chopped ½ inch
Salt & pepper
4 Tablespoons butter
1 teaspoon fresh parsley, minced

DIRECTIONS

STEP ONE
Using a blender or food processor, add all of the crepe batter ingredients and process until smooth. Set batter aside in refrigerator for about 15 minutes or make in advance.

STEP TWO
In a large skillet over medium heat, melt 2 Tablespoons butter and add onions. Cook until caramelized about 20 minutes. Add potato to cook with the onions for the last 7 minutes of cooking time. You could also add the bacon if it has not been previously cooked. Cook until entire mixture is golden brown and crispy.

STEP THREE
In a large skillet or crepe pan, melt ½ Tablespoon of butter over high heat. Pour in about 4 Tablespoons of crepe batter and swirl pan to coat bottom. Allow to cook until bubbles have burst and batter starts to dry. Flip and cook other side until golden brown but not crisp. Put on a large plate and top with a sheet or parchment or waxed paper. Proceed as before until you have used up all the batter. (These can be frozen up to 2 months, or drizzle with fresh lemon juice and sugar as dessert!)

STEP FOUR
Lower heat to medium. Lay out crepe in pan and fill with 1/3 cup of onion mixture and top with 2—3 Tablespoons grated raclette cheese. Fold each side in until you make a square, leaving filling exposed. Once cheese has melted, remove from heat, garnish with parsley and serve immediately!

Other Filling Ideas

- *Mushrooms, spinach & fontina cheese*
- *Ham, fried egg & gruyere cheese*
- *Smoked salmon, capers & cream cheese*
  (I add fresh dill to these!)
- *Chicken, asparagus & feta cheese*
- *Tomatoes, basil leaves & fresh mozzarella*
- *Proscuitto, fresh pear slices, & brie cheese*
- *Nutella & bananas sauteed in butter*

BAKED EGGS (SHIRRED EGGS)

INGREDIENTS

Softened butter for greasing ramekins
4 large eggs
4 Tablespoons heavy cream
2 Tablespoons Gruyere cheese, grated
Salt & pepper
4 teaspoons fresh herbs, minced

DIRECTIONS

STEP ONE
Preheat oven to 375 degrees and grease 4 small ramekins.

STEP TWO
In each ramekin add egg. Pour 1 Tablespoon of heavy cream over the egg, add a pinch of the gruyere cheese and a pinch of the fresh herbs. Add salt and pepper to taste.

STEP THREE
Bake 10-12 minutes until yolk reaches your desired consistency. My preference is to have the white set but the yolk still a bit wobbly and runny. For the firmest eggs, bake 15 minutes. Serve with a lovely crusty bread and green salad!

MUSHROOM TART

SERVINGS: 6

INGREDIENTS

1 10 inch pie crust, homemade or purchased
2 Tablespoons extra virgin olive oil
4 Tablespoons butter
1 ½ cups onions, ½ inch dice
1 Tablespoon minced garlic
8 ounces fresh mushrooms
   (a variety of types is best) **sliced**

1 teaspoon salt
1 teaspoon pepper
8 ounces cream cheese
1 cup heavy cream
2 cups fontina cheese, shredded
3 Tablespoons fresh chives, chopped
2 T fresh thyme, leaves removed from stems

DIRECTIONS

STEP ONE
Preheat oven to 350 degrees.
Use an 8-10 inch tart pan with removable bottom. Line pan with pie dough and press into sides of pan. Trim top edges and prick bottom of dough. Blind bake for 15 minutes.

STEP TWO
In a large skillet over medium heat, combine olive oil and butter, add onion, garlic and mushrooms. Cook until onions are tender and translucent.

STEP THREE
Add cream cheese, heavy cream and fontina cheese. Cook until all cheese is fully melted. Add fresh herbs and stir to combine. Pour mixture into prepared crust.

STEP FOUR
Bake 35 minutes until filling is set and golden brown. Garnish with an additional bundle of thyme and parmigiano cheese curls.

APPALACHIAN SLAW

SERVINGS: 4

INGREDIENTS

4 cups finely chopped cabbage, green and red
1 tomato, diced
½ cucumber, diced
½ cup onion, diced
1 Tablespoon sugar
1 Tablespoon mayonnaise
1 Tablespoon apple cider vinegar
Salt & pepper to taste

DIRECTIONS

In a large bowl, combine sugar, mayonnaise, vinegar, salt and pepper. Add vegetables and stir to thoroughly combine. Allow to rest at least an hour in the refrigerator and gently toss again before serving.

SIMPLE VINAIGRETTE
WITH ENDLESS POSSIBILITIES

YIELD: 1/2 CUP

INGREDIENTS

1 teaspoon French mustard, whole grain or Dijon
Salt & pepper to taste
1 teaspoon honey
2 Tablespoons vinegar OR choice — Champagne, Balsamic, Red Wine, Sherry
1/3 cup extra virgin olive oil, best quality you can afford

DIRECTIONS

Combine all ingredients in a small glass jar with airtight lid and shake until emulsified. Taste and adjust seasonings. Use immediately or store refrigerated up to 7 days.

This recipe has endless possibilities of flavors!

ROASTED GARLIC ASPARAGUS

SERVINGS: 4

INGREDIENTS

2 pounds fresh asparagus, trimmed
1/4 cup olive oil
4-6 cloves garlic, minced
1 lemon, zested and cut into 4 quarters
1 teaspoons lemon zest
1 teaspoon dried oregano
¼ teaspoon red pepper flakes
Salt & pepper to taste
½ cup feta cheese, crumbled

DIRECTIONS

STEP ONE
In a small saucepan heat olive oil, garlic, lemon zest, oregano and red pepper flakes over low heat. Cook until garlic just begins to brown. Remove from heat.

STEP TWO
Preheat oven to 475 degrees.

STEP THREE
On a rimmed baking sheet, toss asparagus with the olive oil mixture until well coated. Arrange asparagus in a single layer. Season with salt and pepper. Roast in oven 10-12 minutes until asparagus has reached desired tenderness.

STEP FOUR
Squeeze lemon juice over asparagus. Transfer to serving platter, sprinkle with feta and serve. Squeeze lemon juice over asparagus. Transfer to serving platter, sprinkle with feta and serve.

WARM GARLIC POTATO SALAD

SERVINGS: 2

INGREDIENTS

4 medium potatoes, Yukon gold or red skin, cut into 1 inch cubes
¾ cup mayonnaise, I prefer Duke's
4 cloves garlic, minced finely or pressed
1-2 Tablespoons Pedro Ximenez Sherry Vinegar
2 scallions, cleaned and sliced thin
1 Tablespoon fresh Italian parsley, minced
Salt & pepper

DIRECTIONS

STEP ONE
In a large saucepan over high heat, bring water and potatoes to a boil and cook 12 minutes until fork tender, drain potatoes.

STEP TWO
In a large bowl, combine mayonnaise, vinegar, garlic, scallions, parsley, salt and pepper. Stir to combine, then taste and adjust any seasonings.

STEP THREE
Gently stir in potatoes and allow to rest about 10 minutes. Stir again so potatoes are completely covered in sauce and serve.

WINTER SALAD

INGREDIENTS

Butter lettuce
Blue cheese *(I like Roquefort)*
Pickled red onions
Pecans, toasted, and broken into pieces

DIRECTIONS

Tear lettuce into large pieces and top with desired amount of blue cheese, onions and nuts.

CREAMY HERB DRESSING

INGREDIENTS

1/3 cup buttermilk
1 teaspoon lemon juice
Zest from 1 lemon
1 clove garlic, minced
½ cup fresh herbs, minced
Salt & pepper

DIRECTIONS

Combine all ingredients and stir well. Allow to sit 15 minutes or more to enhance flavor. This can be made ahead and stored up to 6 days in the refrigerator.

SWEET PICKLED RED ONIONS

SERVINGS: APPROX 2 QUARTS

INGREDIENTS

2 ½ lbs medium red onions
5 cups distilled white vinegar
2 ½ cups sugar
2 cinnamon sticks, 6 inches each
6 whole cloves
8 whole allspice berries
2 dried chilies, small
2 whole star anise
4 dried bay leaves
8 whole black peppercorns

DIRECTIONS

STEP ONE
Trim the ends off the onions, peel away the papery layers and slice into 1/3 inch thick rounds.

STEP TWO
In a large stock pot place remaining ingredients over medium heat and bring to a boil. Add about on third of the onions to the boiling liquid and allow it to come to a boil again. When liquid is back to boiling point, remove the onion slices and place on a baking sheet to cool. Follow the same process for the remaining fresh onion slices.

STEP THREE
Do the above boiling and cooling a total of 3 times.

STEP FOUR
Once you've removed the onions for the third time, allow liquid to boil and reduce the liquid by about half. It will be thick and slightly pink.

STEP FIVE
I like to use a large glass jar with a hinge lid to store my slices. Split onions and liquid evenly between jars, onions should be fully immersed in liquid Store refrigerated. The liquid can also be used in vinaigrettes.

PRESERVING YOUR HERBS

STEP ONE
Cut fresh herbs of choice and remove all leaves from stems. Thyme can be left on the stem. Wash and pat dry.

STEP TWO
Set microwave on highest setting. Lay leaves on a paper towel leaving at least ¼ inch between each one.

STEP THREE
Microwave 30 seconds for the smallest lightest leaves and up to 1 minute for heavier larger leaves. Leaves will curl slightly but stay green and become brittle.

STEP FOUR
Leave leaves whole and place in an airtight jar. Don't forget to note the date on the jar! Crumble leaves when you need to use them for the freshest flavor.

QUICK PICKLED RED CABBAGE

YEILD 1/2 GALLON

INGREDIENTS

1 small head red cabbage, cored and sliced 1/8 inch thick
4 cups apple cider vinegar
4 Tablespoons best balsamic vinegar
4 Tablespoons best red or white wine vinegar
4 bay leaves
¼ cup sea salt

This pickled cabbage recipe is a bit more English by nature. It tastes amazing on salads, cold meats, hummus and served with cheeses.

DIRECTIONS

STEP ONE
Remove outer leaves of cabbage and core. Slice into thin, 1/8 inch thick slices and place in a large colander in sink. Sprinkle evenly with salt, mixing thoroughly. Allow to drain about 15 minutes, occasionally pressing with your hands or spoon.

STEP TWO
Wash jar(s) and lid(s) in hot soapy water and rinse well. Pack cabbage tightly into jar and place a bay leaf in each one.

STEP THREE
In a large pitcher or measuring cup, mix vinegars. Pour to fill each jar to cover cabbage. Use a knife or handle of spoon and slide down inside of jar to remove air bubbles. Do this 3-4 times until no more bubbles rise to the top. If you run out of vinegar and cabbage is not covered, you can add some water.

STEP FOUR
Place in refrigerator to rest. Stores up to 6 months refrigerated.

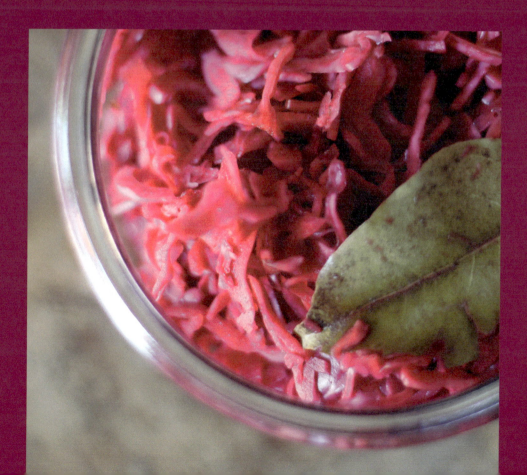

TUSCAN PORK TENDERLOIN

SERVINGS: 4

INGREDIENTS

- 4 Tablespoon garlic, minced
- 4 Tablespoon fresh Italian parsley, minced
- 4 Tablespoons fresh basil, minced
- 1 teaspoon coarse sea salt
- 1 teaspoon ground pepper
- ¼ cup extra virgin olive oil
- 2 lb pork tenderloin, tendon removed and ends trimmed
- Cooking twine or skewers

DIRECTIONS

STEP ONE
In a small bowl combine garlic, herbs, salt and pepper with 1 Tablespoon of the olive oil.

STEP TWO
Pat tenderloin dry and lay on a flat surface. To filet the tenderloin, you will make only 3 cuts running lengthwise. You will want to cut about ¾ of the way through the tenderloin. Using a very sharp knife, make first cut about 1/3 of the way toward the top, open it flat against surface and make another cut 1/3 way from the bottom. If necessary, your 3rd cut will be to even out any areas that are too thin.

STEP THREE
Cover inside of flattened tenderloin with herb mixture and roll up. Secure with twine or cooking skewers.

STEP FOUR
Rub a small amount of olive oil on exterior.

STEP FIVE
OVEN METHOD: Preheat oven to 400 degrees. In a large saute pan over high heat, sear seam side down first, the turn twice to sear add sides of the tenderloin. Move directly to preheated oven and bake 15 minutes. Remove from oven, cover pan with foil and allow to rest for 5 minutes.

GRILL METHOD: Preheat grill to 500 degrees. Place tenderloin seam side down and sear each side. Reduce grill flame to low and cook an additional 12 minutes. Remove and cover with tin foil for 5 minutes.

STEP SEVEN
To finish, remove twine or skewers, carve into 1 inch slices and drizzle with your best quality extra virgin olive oil.

Montalcino & Val d'Orcia in September. Vineyards, olives and crops amongst the hills and sun. Stunning views, wine and food!

EPI ROLLS WITH COMPOUND BUTTER

YIELD: 16 ROLLS

INGREDIENTS

ROLLS
1 ¼ cup hot tap water
3 cups all purpose flour
1 Tablespoon instant yeast
2 teaspoons sea salt

DOUGH WASH
2 Tablespoons butter, melted
1 teaspoon poppy seeds
1 Tablespoon shallot, finely chopped
½ teaspoon sea salt

COMPOUND BUTTER
8 ounces salted butter, very soft
2 Tablespoons fresh herbs, finely chopped

DIRECTIONS (ROLLS)

STEP ONE
In a stand mixer with dough hook attached, combine all roll ingredients and set mixer to low. Allow a few minutes for dough to come together. Once it has formed a ball on the hook, allow to knead for 5 minutes. The dough should look shiny and be stretchy. Cover mixing bowl with a towel and allow to rise about 15 minutes in a draft free place.

STEP TWO
Turn dough out of bowl onto a floured surface and divide in half. Using your hands, stretch dough into a 3 by 10 inch rectangle that is relatively even in thickness. Roll dough up lengthwise into a baguette. Place on a parchment lined baking sheet. Do the same process for other half of dough.

STEP THREE
Using a sharp pair of kitchen scissors, snip equal portions of dough at a sharp angle leaving only ½ inch of dough connecting all pieces. As you make each snip, lay that portion of dough to opposite side of the one before it. It will resemble a sheaf of wheat. Cover dough with a clean towel and allow to rise 15 minutes as your oven preheats.

STEP FOUR
Preheat oven to 375 degrees.

STEP FIVE (DOUGH WASH)
In a small bowl combine:
2 Tablespoons butter, melted
1 teaspoon poppy seeds
1 Tablespoon shallot, finely chopped
½ teaspoon sea salt

STEP SIX
Brush the risen rolls generously with butter mixture using all of it.

STEP SEVEN
Bake 25 minutes until deep golden brown and slightly hollow sounding when tapped.

DIRECTIONS (COMPOUND BUTTER)

STEP ONE
Mix ingredients together until completely combined. Scoop the mixture onto a sheet of plastic wrap and gently form into desired shape. You could use a dish to mold it or just form into a roll style.

STEP TWO
Allow butter to chill about 30 minutes in the refrigerator. Remove plastic wrap and garnish the exterior shape with a full herb leaf, assorted seeds or edible flowers. Cover again with plastic wrap and refrigerate until very firm.

CHICKEN WITH 40 GARLIC CLOVES
SAUTE DE POULET AUX QUARANTE GOUSSES D'AIL
SERVINGS: 4

INGREDIENTS

4 pounds chicken breast meat, cut into cutlets OR 8 chicken thighs
Salt & pepper
3 Tablespoons butter
4 cloves garlic, minced
½ cup white wine vinegar *(Champagne vinegar recommended)*
1 cup chicken stock
1 Bouquet Garni *(a bundle of dried herbs)*

DIRECTIONS

STEP ONE
Pat chicken pieces dry with a paper towel and season both sides with salt and pepper.

STEP TWO
In a large heavy skillet over medium high heat, melt 1 Tablespoon butter. Add chicken to pan and brown one side about 7 minutes, turn once and brown about 4 minutes.

STEP THREE
Turn heat to low, add garlic and allow to brown to just golden. Add vinegar, stock and bouquet garni to pan. Increase stove temperature to medium and allow pan juices to reduce, it takes about 10-15 minutes. Sauce should be slightly thickened and concentrated.

STEP FOUR
Remove chicken from pan and tent with foil. Remove bouquet garni and discard. At a brisk simmer add remaining butter by the Tablespoon, whisking until incorporated fully before adding the next. Once butter is fully incorporated, spoon sauce over chicken and serve immediately. Garnish with minced fresh parsley. The sauce should have substance with a silky and thin texture.

COD IN WINE SAUCE WITH CAPERS & SHALLOTS

SERVINGS: 4

INGREDIENTS

1 fresh lemon
4 cod fillets
Salt & pepper to taste
1 Tablespoon shallot, finely chopped
6 Tablespoons unsalted butter
1 Tablespoon capers, rinsed
½ cup dry white wine, preferably unoaked
Finely chopped fresh Italian parsley for garnish

DIRECTIONS

STEP ONE
Cut the lemon in half. Squeeze juice of one of the halves into a small bowl and set aside. Chop remaining lemon into wedges and put aside until ready to serve.

STEP TWO
Season fish fillets with salt and pepper.

STEP THREE
In a large skillet over medium heat, melt 4 Tablespoons of butter. When the butter stops foaming, add shallots and cook for 1 minute. Add the fish fillets and capers. Cook until golden brown then flip and cook until fully cooked, about 4 minutes. Add the wine and cook an additional 3 minutes. Remove fillets from pan and plate them.

STEP FOUR
Lower the heat under skillet to medium and swirl in the remaining 2 Tablespoons of butter. When butter has melted but is not foaming, add lemon juice and stir to combine. Taste sauce and adjust seasonings.

STEP FIVE
Pour sauce over each piece of fish and garnish with parsley. Serve with lemon wedges on the side

GRILLED TURKEY BURGERS WITH SMOKEY AIOLI

SERVINGS: 4

INGREDIENTS

½ cup mayonnaise
½ teaspoon cumin
½ teaspoon coriander seeds or ground
2 Tablespoons extra virgin olive oil
2 teaspoons lemon juice
1 ½ teaspoons smoked paprika
1 clove garlic, minced or pressed
Salt & pepper

1 pound ground turkey
1 large red pepper, cleaned and cut into ½ inch thick slice
4 slices sharp white cheddar
1 large onion, peeled and cut into 1/3 inch thick slices
Handful of fresh mixed greens
4 sesame hamburger buns

DIRECTIONS

AIOLI
STEP ONE
In a small bowl, whisk together mayonnaise, olive oil, lemon juice and spices. Season to taste with salt and pepper.

STEP TWO
In a large bowl mix together ground turkey and 2 tablespoons of aioli mixture. Split meat into 4 equal portions and shape each into a patty. Brush with olive oil, salt and pepper.

STEP THREE
Preheat grill to medium high heat.

STEP FOUR
Brush vegetables with olive oil, salt and pepper.

STEP FIVE
Grill vegetables until soft and slightly charred about 4 minutes per side.

STEP SIX
Grill turkey burgers 5 minutes. Allow to sear until meat releases from the grill grates, turn over and cook an additional 4 minutes. Top with vegetables and slice of cheese and allow turkey to cook through and cheese to melt, about 4 more minutes. Remove from grill, allow to cool 2-3 minutes. Place on bun, top with a dollop of aioli and fresh greens.

PASTA ALLA NORCINA

INGREDIENTS

14oz penne or other short pasta
2-3 Italian pork sausages, casings removed and crumbled
1 yellow onion, sliced fine
1-2 black truffles *(I used 2 small ones)* OR 3 Tablespoons truffle zest
3/4 cup + 2 Tablespoons fresh cream
1/3-1/2 cup dry white wine
2 cup pecorino toscano cheese grated
3-4 tbsp extra virgin olive oil
Salt and black pepper

DIRECTIONS

STEP ONE
Bring a large pot of salted water to a boil for the pasta. Meanwhile, heat the oil in a large frying pan or skillet over a medium heat. Add the onion and cook until it starts to soften then add the crumbled sausage meat.

STEP TWO
Brown the sausage and pour in the wine. Allow the alcohol to evaporate while stirring. Pour in the cream and bring the sauce to a gentle simmer. Add salt and pepper. Add a few truffle shavings (if using) and half the pecorino. Reduce the sauce for 3-4 minutes, then turn off the heat, cover and set aside.

STEP THREE
Cook the pasta in the salted boiling water until al dente according to the instructions on the packet. Save some of the pasta cooking water and drain the pasta.

STEP FOUR
Over a low heat, mix the pasta and sauce together. You can add a little pasta cooking water if it seems too thick.

STEP FIVE
Serve immediately with a generous sprinkling of grated pecorino, some freshly ground black pepper and truffle shavings.

I was so fortunate to experience a bucket list day near San Gimignano Tuscany and take part in a truffle hunt. It was a scorching September day to hike nearly a mile through chianti vineyards to a shaded, dry riverbed with our Italian guide and his 4 dogs. As each dog alerted the guide, he would take a small shovel and carefully break up the soil to expose the white truffle growing on tree roots. The scent of truffles and ripe grapes scented the air as we hiked amongst fallen limbs, drying leaves and a playful pack of dogs.

CHICKEN & MUSHROOM MEAT PIES WITH DEMI GLACE SAUCE

SERVINGS: 6

INGREDIENTS

- 3 Tablespoons olive oil
- 1 1/2 pounds chicken, boneless & skinless, diced into 1/2 inch pieces; raw or cooked
- 2 medium leeks, sliced into 1/8 inch, cleaned well
- ½ cup mushrooms, assorted styles, chopped in ½ inch pieces
- 1 Tablespoon butter
- 1 Tablespoon all purpose flour
- 2 ½ cups chicken stock, hot
- 1 Tablespoon parsley, finely minced
- ½ teaspoon fresh thyme, stems removed
- Salt & pepper
- ½ cup dry white wine — Chablis or Vin de Pays
- 1 sheet puff pastry, defrosted
- 1 egg, beaten for glazing

DIRECTIONS

STEP ONE
Preheat oven to 400 degrees. Lightly oil 6-8 ramekins.

STEP TWO
Heat olive oil in a large saute pan over medium heat and cook chicken about 5 minutes or until browned on all sides. Remove chicken from pan and set aside. Add the leeks and mushrooms to pan and cook for 3 minutes or until leeks are softened. Remove from pan, add it to the chicken that is resting.

STEP THREE
Pour wine into pan to deglaze it, scraping up all the bits. Add butter and allow to melt. Slowly whisk in the flour until smooth and then pour in the hot stock whisking constantly until a smooth gravy has formed. Cook for 3 minutes stirring constantly until mixture has thickened slightly and cooked through. Return chicken, leeks and mushrooms to the pan, add herbs, salt, pepper and continue to cook another 3 minutes until warmed through.

STEP FOUR
Divide filling between ramekins. On a lightly floured surface, unfold puff pastry. Using a rolling pin, roll to 1/8 inch thickness. Cut dough into 6-8 equal size square. Top each ramekin with a square of pastry allowing the sides to drape over the rim of dishes. Brush with the beaten egg and garnish with a bit of remaining parsley, ground black pepper, poppy seeds or bits of leftover puff pastry. Bake 20-25 minutes or until puff pastry is puffed and deep golden brown.

DEMI GLACE SAUCE

INGREDIENTS

- 2 packages Veal demi glace brand
  (I use "More Than Gourmet 1.5 oz")
- ½ - ¾ cup water
- 2 Tablespoons all purpose flour
- 1 Tablespoon butter

DIRECTIONS

STEP ONE
In a saute pan over medium heat, melt butter. Stir in flour whisking until smooth. Allow flour to brown stirring constantly. Add water and demi glace and whisk until very smooth and gravy has thickened. You can add more water if needed. The consistency of this gravy should be slightly thinner than a traditional gravy, more sauce like and less gelatinous.

STEP TWO
Serve pies along with steamed vegetables and a healthy drizzle of gravy.

GARLIC GINGER SHRIMP LINGUINE

SERVINGS: 4

INGREDIENTS

1 pound shrimp, raw, peeled, deveined
2 Tablespoon extra virgin olive oil
4 Tablespoons fresh ginger, peeled and grated or minced
7 cloves garlic, minced
2 cups dry white wine — Chablis or Vin de Pays
Salt & pepper
4 Tablespoons basil, sliced into thin ribbons
½ lb Linguine pasta, cooked al dente

DIRECTIONS

STEP ONE
Rinse shrimp and pat dry with a paper towel.

STEP TWO
In a very large skillet, heat olive oil to hot (but not smoking) over high heat. Add 3 Tablespoons of the ginger, garlic, salt and pepper to oil. Cook 2-3 minutes until garlic is just turning golden brown. Add the wine and cook until reduced to about 1 cup, around 8 minutes.

STEP THREE
Add all of the shrimp in a single layer and continue cooking about 4 minutes until shrimp turn pink.

STEP FOUR
Remove pan from heat and add linguine to the pan. Toss lightly to coat the pasta then garnish with remaining ginger and basil. Adjust the salt and pepper to taste and serve immediately.

STICKY TOFFEE PUDDING

SERVINGS: 8

Cake

INGREDIENTS
- 7 Tablespoons butter, softened
- ¾ cup brown sugar
- 2 large eggs
- 1 cup self rising flour
- 1 teaspoon baking powder
- 1 teaspoon baking soda
- 3 Tablespoons molasses, black strap, dark or treacle syrup
- 1 ¼ cup whole milk

DIRECTIONS
STEP ONE
Preheat oven to 350 degrees and grease a 9x9 inch baking pan. In a mixing bowl, combine all ingredients except milk. Whip with flat beater about 30 seconds or until combined.

STEP TWO
Pour in the milk and whisk again until just combined. This will be a very loose batter. Pour into prepared pan and bake 35-40 minutes until well risen and springy. Cake will pull away slightly from edges.

Toffee Sauce

INGREDIENTS
- 7 Tablespoons butter
- 2/3 cup brown sugar
- 1 Tablespoon molasses
- 1 ¼ cups heavy cream
- 1 teaspoon vanilla extract OR
  - 1 vanilla bean split and paste removed

DIRECTIONS
STEP ONE
Pour all ingredients in a small sauce pan and set over low heat. Stir until the sugar has dissolved and butter has melted.

STEP TWO
Bring to a boil and boil 1 minute stirring continuously. Set aside to cool. This can be stored in the refrigerator up to 3 days.

Custard

INGREDIENTS
- 2 cups milk
- ¼ cup heavy cream
- 4 large egg yolks
- 2 Tablespoons sugar
- 2 Tablespoons cornstarch
- 2 Tablespoons vanilla extract OR
  - 2 vanilla beans split and paste removed

DIRECTIONS
STEP ONE
In a small saucepan over low heat, bring milk and cream to a simmer.

STEP TWO
In a mixing bowl, whisk in egg yolks, sugar and cornstarch until thick and pale. Remove milk from heat and add ½ cup or so of egg mixture to milk, whisking until combined to temper the mixture.

STEP THREE
Add remaining egg mixture and whisk until fully incorporated. Return the saucepan to low heat and cook until thickened. It should coat the back of a spoon.

STEP FOUR
Top a slice of cake with a generous amount of toffee sauce and then top with a small amount of custard. This is always best served warm.

VICTORIA SPONGE CAKE

SERVINGS: 14

SPONGE CAKE

INGREDIENTS

1 cup unsalted butter, softened
¾ cup sugar
1 teaspoon vanilla extract
4 large eggs
1 1/3 cup self rising flour
2 Tablespoons corn starch
¼ teaspoon salt
3-4 Tablespoons milk
8 ounces raspberry jam, use the best quality
Buttercream frosting or fresh whipped cream

SELF RISING FLOUR
1 cup all purpose flour
1 ½ teaspoons baking powder
½ teaspoon salt

DIRECTIONS

STEP ONE
Preheat oven to 350 degrees. Grease and flour (2) 8-9 inch round pans.

STEP TWO
In a large mixing bowl, combine all ingredients except milk. Beat with an electric mixer at low until combined then raise the speed to medium. Beat 3-5 minutes until batter is fluffy and holds soft peaks. Add milk and beat until fully combined. Divide batter evenly between prepared pans.

STEP THREE
Bake 25 minutes until edges pull away from pan and cake is a light golden brown. Cool cakes for 10 minutes in a pan then gently turn out onto a cake rack to fully cool.

STEP FOUR
To finish the cakes, cut each cake layer in half and take 2 layers and evenly spread them with jam. Spread the other 2 layers with buttercream frosting.

STEP FIVE
Begin assembling with 1 layer of jam covered cake on a plate. Next, sandwich 1 jam and 1 buttercream layer together with ingredients facing each other and place a plain layer on the top. Spread remaining buttercream on top of cake and decorate with fresh raspberries or a swirl of remaining jam.

BUTTERCREAM FROSTING

INGREDIENTS

1 cup unsalted butter, soft
3-4 cups powdered sugar
1 Tablespoon vanilla extract
Up to 4 Tablespoons milk

DIRECTIONS

STEP ONE
In a large mixing bowl, using a flat beater, beat butter on medium speed for 3-5 minutes until pale and fluffy. Add 3 cups of sugar and continue to beat on medium.

STEP TWO
Add in vanilla extract and beat an additional 3 minutes. As you are beating, adjust the consistency with milk until it looks light and fluffy and still remains sticky and spreadable.

Other Fun Ideas

- Poke holes in warm cake and drizzle evenly with 2 tablespoons of elderflower liqueur. Serve topped with fresh sliced strawberries and whipped cream.

- Add 1 tablespoon instant espresso powder to the uncooked batter. Serve topped with a simple chocolate ganache or hot fudge sauce and whipped cream.

- Fill layers with Nutella and sliced bananas. Top cake with a layer of Nutella and chopped toasted hazelnuts.

- Replace vanilla extract with almond extract in uncooked batter. Fill with cherry pie filling and drizzle with a powdered sugar/lemon zest glaze.

DECADENT FUDGE BROWNIES

SERVINGS: 8-16

INGREDIENTS

1 cup butter
2 cups sugar
4 large eggs
¾ cup cocoa powder
("natural" undutched achieves fudgiest results)
2/3 cup all purpose flour
½ teaspoon baking powder
1 Tablespoon vanilla extract
1 teaspoon sea salt
(reduce to ½ teaspoon if using salted butter)

DIRECTIONS

STEP ONE
Preheat oven to 350 degrees. Line a 9 inch square baking pan with aluminum foil so bottom and sides are mostly covered.

STEP TWO
In a small bowl, combine dry ingredients. In a medium bowl, add eggs and beat until foamy and thick.

STEP THREE
In a large saucepan over medium heat, melt butter. When butter has melted, stir in the sugar until completely combined. Remove pan from heat. Add the eggs and whisk until completely combined. Add vanilla extract and stir well.

STEP FOUR
Add the dry ingredients and whisk very slowly until well incorporated. Spread batter into prepared pan and tap to even up the batter.

STEP FIVE
Bake 40 minutes until a toothpick in center comes out clean or with just a few crumbs remaining. Allow to completely cool in pan. When cooled turn out onto a serving dish, carefully peel off the foil liner and cut evenly into 8 or up to 16 pieces

WARM STRAWBERRY RICE PUDDING

SERVINGS: 4

INGREDIENTS

¾ cup coconut milk
¾ cup heavy cream
1 cup Arborio or Bomba rice
½ cup sugar
1 vanilla bean, split & deseeded or 1 teaspoon vanilla extract
Pinch of salt
1 cup strawberries, hulled and cut into quarters
Zest of 1 lemon
½ cup Marcona almonds, coarsely chopped

Notes

DIRECTIONS

STEP ONE
In a large saucepan over high heat, combine rice, milks, sugar and vanilla. Stir to combine and bring to a boil. Reduce heat to a gentle simmer and cover. Cook 30 minutes.

STEP TWO
After 30 minutes, check rice for tenderness and liquid absorption and add strawberries. Set timer up to 10 additional minutes if rice needs a bit more time and liquid still remains. Once you're happy with the tenderness and consistency, remove from heat and fluff gently. Fold in lemon zest. If pudding seems too thick you can add a few tablespoons of heavy cream.

STEP THREE
Serve rice warm with chopped marcona almonds as a garnish.

SCONES

SERVINGS: 8

INGREDIENTS

2 cups all purpose flour
1/3 cup granulated sugar
1 Tablespoon baking powder
6 Tablespoons cold butter
¾ cup heavy cream
2 egg yolks
1 vanilla bean or 2 teaspoons vanilla extract
1 large egg
1 Tablespoon water
1 teaspoon raw sugar

DIRECTIONS

STEP ONE
Preheat oven to 400 degrees.

STEP TWO
In a large bowl add flour, sugar and baking powder. Cut butter into dry ingredients using a pastry cutter or two knives, until mixture resembles coarse crumbs. Mix cream, egg yolks and vanilla together. Pour cream mixture into flour mixture and fold gently with a rubber spatula or a fork until just incorporated. Use a gently touch for light and flaky scones, "and extra mixing will yield a more (English style) dense scone.

STEP THREE
Beat egg and water together until frothy.

STEP FOUR
Lightly flour a flat surface and pat into an 8 inch round about ½ inch thick. Cut into pie wedges and place on a parchment line baking sheet. Brush with egg wash mixture and sprinkle with raw sugar.

STEP FIVE
Bake 18-22 minutes until golden brown.

ADDITIONS

You can always add 1 cup dried fruit to these and they turn out fantastic! I often add dried cherries and swap almond extract for the vanilla bean.

EARL GREY SHORTBREAD COOKIES

INGREDIENTS

4 Tablespoons Earl Grey or your favorite black tea blend
4 cups all purpose flour
1 teaspoon sea salt
1 ½ cups powdered sugar
2 cups unsalted butter, room temperature

DIRECTIONS

STEP ONE
In a large mixing bowl combine all dry ingredients and whisk until incorporated.

STEP TWO
In another large mixing bowl, using an electric mixer, whip butter for 30 seconds on medium speed. Turn speed to low and add the dry ingredients. The dough will slowly form as you continue to mix. It will become thick, clump on the beaters and form a ball. Gather up any small bits left behind.

STEP THREE
Using a large piece of plastic wrap, form a log with the dough, wrap in plastic and roll on counter gently to become even.

STEP FOUR
Refrigerate 30 minutes or longer.

STEP FIVE
Preheat oven to 375 degrees.

STEP SIX
Line a baking sheet with parchment paper. Cut the cookie dough into 1/3 inch thick coins and space evenly on sheet. Bake 12 minutes or until edges are golden brown and dough is set. Allow to cool 10 minutes on baking sheet and then transfer to a cooling rack to cool completely. Store in a sealed container.

INDEX

Crostini with Smoked Fresh Mozzarella & Arugula 6
French-Inspired Charcuterie Board 8
British-Inspired Charcuterie Board 9
Alpine Cheese Dip 10
Goat Cheese Bacon Cranberry Dip 11
Pimm's Cup 12
Limoncello Spritz 12
Lillet Vive 13
Maple Old Fashioned 14
French Orchard Spritz 14
Fancy Ice Cubes 15
Roasted Pumpkin Soup 16
Salmorejo 17
Savory Crepes 18
Baked Eggs 20
Mushroom Tart 21
Appalachian Slaw 22
Simple Vinaigrette 22
Roasted Garlic Asparagus 23
Warm Garlic Potato Salad 23
Winter Salad 24
Sweet Pickled Red Onions 25
Preserving Your Herbs 26
Quick Pickled Red Cabbage 27
Tuscan Pork Tenderloin 28
Epi Rolls with Compound Butter 30
Chicken with 40 Garlic Cloves 32
Cod in Wine Sauce with Capers & Shallots 23
Grilled Turkey Burgers with Smoked Aioli 34
Pasta Alla Norcina 35
Chicken & Mushroom Meat Pies 36
Garlic Ginger Shrimp Linguine 37
Sticky Toffee Pudding 38
Victoria Sponge Cake with Buttercream Frosting 40
Decadent Fudge Brownies 42
Warm Strawberry Rice Pudding 43
Scones 45
Earl Grey Shortbread Cookies 46

Made in the USA
Columbia, SC
16 November 2024